To: Dear Amie

Love
From: Auntie
Susie xo

WISDOM FROM

PEACE IS EVERY STEP

The Path of Mindfulness in Everyday Life

Thich Nhat Hanh

Peter Pauper Press, Inc.
White Plains, New York

The text in this book is excerpted from *Peace Is Every Step: The Path of Mindfulness in Everyday Life* by Thich Nhat Hanh, originally published by Bantam Books, a division of Bantam Doubleday Dell Publishing Group, Inc. Copyright © 1991 by Thich Nhat Hanh. Cover art © 2005, 1991 by Patricia Curtan.

Designed by Karine Syvertsen

Published in 2005 by arrangement with The Bantam Dell Publishing Group, a division of Random House, Inc.

Peter Pauper Press, Inc.
202 Mamaroneck Avenue
White Plains, NY 10601
All rights reserved
ISBN 1-59359-907-2
Printed in China
7 6 5 4 3 2 1

Visit us at www.peterpauper.com

WISDOM FROM

PEACE IS EVERY STEP

*The Path of Mindfulness
in Everyday Life*

Contents

Foreword

BY H. H. THE DALAI LAMA

*A*lthough attempting to bring about world peace through the internal transformation of individuals is difficult, it is the only way. Wherever I go, I express this, and I am encouraged that people from many different walks of life receive it well. Peace must first be developed within an individual. And I believe that love, compassion, and altruism are the fundamental basis for peace. Once these qualities are developed within an individual, he or she is then able to create an atmosphere of peace and harmony. This atmosphere can be expanded and extended from the individual to his family, from the family to the community and eventually to the whole world.

Peace Is Every Step *is a guidebook for a journey in exactly this direction. Thich Nhat Hanh begins by teaching mindfulness of breathing and awareness of the small acts of our daily lives, then shows us how to use the benefits of mindfulness and concentration to transform and heal difficult psychological states. Finally he shows us the connection between personal inner peace and peace on Earth. This is a very worthwhile book. It can change individual lives and the life of our society.*

> *Peace is every step.*
> *The shining red sun is my heart.*
> *Each flower smiles with me.*
> *How green, how fresh all that grows.*
> *How cool the wind blows.*
> *Peace is every step.*
> *It turns the endless path to joy.*

THICH NHAT HANH

PART ONE

Breathe! You Are Alive

Twenty-Four Brand-New Hours

*E*very morning, when we wake up, we have twenty-four brand-new hours to live. What a precious gift! We have the capacity to live in a way that these twenty-four hours will bring peace, joy, and happiness to ourselves and others.

Peace is present right here and now, in ourselves and in everything we do and see. The question is whether or not we are in touch with it. We are very good at preparing to live, but not very *good at living. We have difficulty remembering that we are alive in the present moment, the only moment there is for us to be alive.*

This book is an invitation to come back to the present moment and find peace and joy.

The Dandelion Has My Smile

If in our daily lives we can smile, if we can be peaceful and happy, not only we, but everyone will profit. If we really know how to live, what better way to start the day than with a smile? Our smile affirms our awareness and determination to live in peace and joy. The source of a true smile is an awakened mind. Smiling helps you approach the day with gentleness and understanding.

If you have lost your smile and yet are still capable of seeing that a dandelion is keeping it for you, the situation is not too bad. You still have enough mindfulness to see that the smile is there. The dandelion is one member of your community of friends. It is there, quite faithful, keeping your smile for you.

In fact, everything around you is keeping your smile for you. You don't need to feel isolated. You only have to open yourself to the support that is all around you, and in you.

Conscious Breathing

Breathing in and out is very important and enjoyable. Our breathing is the link between our body and our mind. Sometimes our mind is thinking one thing and our body is doing another, and mind and body are not unified. By concentrating on our breathing, "In" and "Out," we bring body and mind back together and become whole again. When we breathe consciously, we recover ourselves completely and encounter life in the present moment.

Present Moment, Wonderful Moment

In our busy society, it is a great fortune to breathe consciously from time to time. There are many exercises we can do to help us breathe consciously. Besides the simple "In-Out" exercise, we can recite these four lines silently as we breathe in and out:

Breathing in, I calm my body.
Breathing out, I smile.
Dwelling in the present moment,
I know this is a wonderful moment!

Thinking Less

While we practice conscious breathing, our thinking will slow down and we can give ourselves a real rest. Most of the time, we think too much, and mindful breathing helps us to be calm, relaxed, and peaceful. It enables us to be in touch with life, which is wonderful in the present moment.

Sitting Anywhere

When you need to slow down and come back to yourself, you do not need to rush home to practice conscious breathing. Wherever you are, you can breathe mindfully. We all need to go back to ourselves from time to time, in order to be able to confront difficulties of life. We can do this in any position; however, the sitting position is the most stable. Breathing mindfully in any position at any time can help you recover yourself.

Sitting Meditation

The most stable posture for meditation is sitting cross-legged on a cushion. The half-lotus and full-lotus positions are excellent for establishing stability of body and mind. Allow your back to be straight, keep your eyes half closed, and fold your hands comfortably on your lap. If you prefer, you can sit in a chair with your feet flat on the floor and your hands resting on your lap. Or you can lie on the floor, on your back, with your legs straight out, a few inches apart, and your arms at your sides, preferably palms up.

We need to practice meditation gently, but steadily, throughout daily life, not wasting a single opportunity or event to see deeply into the true nature of life, including our everyday problems. Practicing in this way, we dwell in profound communion with life.

Bells of Mindfulness

In my tradition, we use the temple bells to remind us to come back to the present moment. Every time we hear the bell, we stop talking, stop our thinking, and return to ourselves, breathing in and out, and smiling. Whatever we are doing, we pause for a moment and just enjoy our breathing. Sometimes we also recite this verse:

Listen, listen.
This wonderful sound brings me
back to my true self.

You can use any sound to remind you to pause, breathe in and out, and enjoy the present moment. Even non-sounds, such as the rays of sunlight coming through the window, are bells of mindfulness that can remind us to return to ourselves, breathe, smile, and live fully in the present moment.

Eating Mindfully

Eating a meal in mindfulness is an important practice. When the food is on the table and everyone is seated, we practice breathing. Then we look at each person as we breathe in and out in order to be in touch with ourselves and everyone at the table. Sitting at the table with other people, we have a chance to offer an authentic smile of friendship and understanding. After breathing and smiling, we look down at the food in a way that allows the food to become real. This food reveals

our connection with the earth.
Contemplating our food for a few
seconds before eating, and eating in
mindfulness, can bring us much
happiness.

Walking Meditation

Walking meditation is to enjoy the walking—walking not in order to arrive, but just to walk. The purpose is to be in the present moment and, aware of our breathing and our walking, to enjoy each step. Therefore we have to shake off all worries and anxieties, not thinking of the future, not thinking of the past, just enjoying the present moment.

Telephone Meditation

The telephone is very convenient, but we can be tyrannized by it. We may find its ring disturbing. The next time you hear the phone ring, stay where you are, breathe in and out consciously, smile to yourself, and recite this verse: "Listen, listen. This wonderful sound brings me back to my true self." When the bell rings for the second time, repeat the verse and your smile will be even more solid. When the phone rings for the third time, continue to practice breathing and smiling as you walk to the phone slowly. Because you have been breathing consciously and smiling, you are dwelling in mindfulness, and when you pick up the phone, how fortunate for the person calling you! Practicing telephone meditation can counteract stress and depression and bring mindfulness into our daily lives.

Driving Meditation

I have written a simple verse you can recite before starting your car:

Before starting the car,
I know where I am going.
The car and I are one.
If the car goes fast, I go fast.

Sometimes we don't really need to use the car, but because we want to get away from ourselves, we go for a drive. We are afraid of being alone with ourselves. We want to escape.

Driving is a daily task in this

society. I am not suggesting you stop driving, just that you do so consciously. While we are driving, we think only about arriving. Therefore, every time we see a red light, we are not very happy. The next time you see a red light, please smile at it and go back to your breathing. Transform a feeling of irritation into a pleasant feeling. Although it is the same red light, it becomes different. It becomes a friend, helping us remember that it is only in the present moment that we can live our lives.

Aimlessness

There is a word in Buddhism that means "wishlessness" or "aimlessness." The idea is that you do not put something in front of you and run after it, because everything is already here, in yourself. While we practice walking meditation, we do not try to arrive anywhere. We only make peaceful, happy steps. By taking good care of the present moment, we take good care of the future.

Our Life Is a Work of Art

If we just act in each moment with composure and mindfulness, each minute of our life is a work of art. Even when we are not painting or writing, we are still creating. If we just act with awareness and integrity, our art will flower, and we don't have to talk about it at all. When we know how to *be* peace, we find that art is a wonderful way to share our peacefulness. Artistic expression will take place in one way or another, but the *being* is essential. So we must go back to ourselves, and when we have joy and peace in ourselves, our creations of art will be quite natural and they will serve the world in a positive way.

Hope as an Obstacle

Hope is important, because it can make the present moment less difficult to bear. If we believe that tomorrow will be better, we can bear a hardship today. But that is the most that hope can do for us—to make some hardship lighter. When I think deeply about the nature of hope, I see something tragic. Since we cling to our hope in the future, we do not focus our energies and capabilities on the present moment. If you can refrain from hoping, you can bring yourself entirely into the present moment and discover the joy that is already here.

There is no way to peace,
peace is the way.

A. J. MUSTE

Breathing Room

I recommend that we set up a small
room in our homes and call it a
"breathing room," where we can be
alone and practice just breathing and
smiling. You may want to have a small
bell, a few cushions, and perhaps a
vase of flowers. Every time you feel
upset, go to that room, open the door
slowly, sit down, invite the bell to
sound, and begin to breathe. I believe
that every home should have one
room for breathing. Simple practices
like conscious breathing and smiling

are very important. They can change our civilization.

The practice of peace and reconciliation is one of the most vital and artistic of all human actions.

Continuing the Journey

We have walked together in mindful-
ness, learning how to breathe and smile
in full awareness throughout the day.
But how can we deal with difficult
emotions? What should we do when we
feel anger, hatred, remorse, or sadness?
Shall we continue our journey together
and try some of these practices?

PART TWO

Transformation and Healing

The River of Feelings

Our feelings play a very important part in directing all of our thoughts and actions. In us, there is a river of feelings, in which every drop of water is a different feeling and each feeling relies on all the others for its existence.

There are three sorts of feelings—pleasant, unpleasant, and neutral. When we have an unpleasant feeling, we may want to chase it away. But it is more effective to return to our conscious breathing and just observe it, identifying it silently to ourselves:

"Breathing in, I know there is an unpleasant feeling in me. Breathing out, I know there is an unpleasant feeling in me."

We can use our breathing to be in contact with our feelings and accept them. If our breathing is light and calm—a natural result of conscious breathing—our mind and body will slowly become light, calm, and clear, and our feelings also. Mindful observation is based on the principle of "nonduality": our feeling is not separate from us or caused merely by something outside us; our feeling *is* us, and for the moment we *are* that feeling.

If we face our unpleasant feelings with care, affection, and nonviolence, we can transform them into the kind of energy that is healthy and has the capacity to nourish us. By the work of mindful observation, our unpleasant feelings can illuminate so much for us, offering us insight and understanding into ourselves and society.

Non-Surgery

We do not need surgery to remove our anger. We only have to observe it with love and attention. If we take care of our anger in this way, without trying to run away from it, it will transform itself. This is peacemaking. If we are peaceful in ourselves, we can make peace with our anger. We can deal with any unpleasant feeling in the same way.

Transforming Feelings

The first step in dealing with feelings is to recognize each feeling as it arises. The agent that does this is mindfulness. In the case of fear, for example, you bring out your mindfulness, look at your fear, and recognize it as fear. You know that fear springs from yourself and that mindfulness also springs from yourself. They are both in you, not fighting, but one taking care of the other.

The second step is to become one with the feeling. Say, "Hello, Fear.

How are you today?" Then you can invite the two aspects of yourself, mindfulness and fear, to shake hands as friends and become one. Doing this may seem frightening, but because you know that you are more than your fear, you need not be afraid. As long as mindfulness is there, it can chaperone your fear. The fundamental practice is to nourish your mindfulness with conscious breathing, to keep it there, alive and strong. As long as mindfulness is present, you will not drown in your fear. In fact, you begin transforming it the very moment you give birth to awareness in yourself.

The third step is to calm the feeling. As mindfulness is taking good care of your fear, you begin to calm it down. "Breathing in, I calm the activities of body and mind." You calm your feeling just by being with it.

The fourth step is to release the feeling, to let it go. Because of your calm, you feel at ease, even in the midst of fear, and you know that your fear will not grow into something that will overwhelm you. Calming and releasing are just medicines for the symptoms. You now have an opportunity to go deeper and work on transforming the source of your fear.

The fifth step is to look deeply. You look deeply into your baby—your feeling of fear—to see what is wrong, even after the baby has already stopped crying, after the fear is gone. You cannot hold your baby all the time, and therefore you have to look into him to see the cause of what is wrong. By looking, you will see what will help you begin to transform the feeling. You will realize, for example, that his suffering has many causes, inside and outside of his body.

Looking into your baby, you see the elements that are causing him to cry, and when you see them, you will know what to do and what not to do to transform the feeling and be free.

After recognizing the feeling, becoming one with it, calming it down, and releasing it, we can look deeply into its causes, which are often based on inaccurate perceptions. As soon as we understand the causes and nature of our feelings, they begin to transform themselves.

Mindfulness of Anger

Anger is an unpleasant feeling. It is like a blazing flame that burns up our self-control and causes us to say and do things that we regret later. Anger and hatred are the materials from which hell is made. A mind without anger is cool, fresh, and sane. The absence of anger is the basis of real happiness, the basis of love and compassion.

When our anger is placed under the lamp of mindfulness, it immediately begins to lose some of its destructive nature. Our awareness of our anger does not suppress it or drive it out. It just looks after it. This is a very important principle. Mindfulness is not a judge. It is more like an older sister looking after and comforting her younger sister in an affectionate and caring way. We can concentrate on our breathing in order to maintain this mindfulness and know ourselves fully.

When we are angry, our anger is our very self. To suppress or chase it away is to suppress or chase away our self. When we are joyful, we are the joy. When we are angry, we are the anger. When anger is born in us, we can be aware that anger is an energy in us, and we can accept that energy in order to transform it into another kind of energy. We know that anger can be a kind of compost, and that it is within its power to give birth to something beautiful. We need anger in the way the organic gardener needs compost. If we know how to accept our anger, we already have some peace and joy. Gradually we can transform anger completely into peace, love, and understanding.

Walking Meditation
When Angry

When anger arises, we may wish to go
outside to practice walking meditation. Practice like this:

> *Breathing in,*
> *I know that anger is here.*
> *Breathing out,*
> *I know that the anger is me.*
> *Breathing in,*
> *I know that anger is unpleasant.*
> *Breathing out,*
> *I know this feeling will pass.*

Breathing in, I am calm.
Breathing out, I am strong enough
to take care of this anger.

To lessen the unpleasant feeling brought about by the anger, we give our whole heart and mind to the practice of walking meditation. As we walk, we recite this verse and wait until we are calm enough to look directly at the anger. After a while, our anger will subside and we will feel stronger. Then we can begin to observe the anger directly and try to understand it.

The Roots of Anger

Anger is rooted in our lack of understanding of ourselves and of the causes, deep-seated as well as immediate, that brought about this unpleasant state of affairs. Anger is also rooted in desire, pride, agitation, and suspicion. The primary roots of our anger are in ourselves. Our environment and other people are only secondary.

Internal Formations

There is a term in Buddhist psychology that can be translated as "internal formations," or "knots." When we have a sensory input, depending on how we receive it, a knot may be tied in us. The way to deal with unconscious internal formations is, first of all, to find ways to become aware of them. By practicing mindful breathing, we may gain access to some of the knots that are tied inside us. When we are aware of our images, feelings, thoughts, words, and behavior, we can ask ourselves questions such as: Why did I feel uncomfortable when I heard him say that? Why did I say that to him? Observing closely like this can gradually bring the internal formations that are buried in us into the realm of the conscious mind.

If we know how to live every moment in an awakened way, we will be aware of what is going on in our feelings and perceptions in the present moment, and we will not let knots form or become tighter in our consciousness. And if we know how to observe our feelings, we can find the

roots of long-standing internal formations and transform them, even those
that have become quite strong.

*The absence of clear
understanding is the basis
for every knot.*

Living Together

When we live with another person, to protect each other's happiness, we should help one another transform the internal formations that we produce together. By practicing understanding and loving speech, we can help each other a great deal. Happiness is no longer an individual matter. If the other person is not happy, we will not be happy either. To transform the other person's knots will help bring about our own happiness as well.

The root cause of any internal

formation is a lack of understanding. To practice mindful observation is to look deeply to be able to see the nature and causes of something. One important benefit of this kind of insight is the untying of our knots.

Suchness

In Buddhism, the word "suchness" is used to mean "the essence or particular characteristics of a thing or a person, its true nature." Each person has his or her suchness. If we want to live in peace and happiness with a person, we have to see the suchness of that person. Once we see it, we understand him or her, and there will be no trouble. We can live peacefully and happily together.

Nourishing Healthy Seeds

Consciousness exists on two levels: as seeds and as manifestations of these seeds. Every time a seed has an occasion to manifest itself, it produces new seeds of the same kind. If we are angry for five minutes, new seeds of anger are produced and deposited in the soil of our unconscious mind.

There are many kinds of seeds in us, both good and bad. Some were planted during our lifetime, and some were transmitted by our parents, our ancestors, and our society. Every time we practice mindful living, we plant healthy seeds and strengthen the healthy seeds already in us. If we plant wholesome, healing, refreshing seeds, they will take care of the negative seeds, even without our asking.

What's Not Wrong?

We often ask, "What's wrong?" Doing so, we invite painful seeds of sorrow to come up and manifest. We feel suffering, anger, and depression, and produce more such seeds. We would be much happier if we tried to stay in touch with the healthy, joyful seeds inside of us and around us. We should learn to ask, "What's not wrong?" and be in touch with that.

Awareness of the precious elements of happiness is itself the practice of right mindfulness. Elements like these are within us and all around us. In each second of our lives we can enjoy them. If we do so, seeds of peace, joy, and happiness will be planted in us, and they will become strong. The secret to happiness is happiness itself. Wherever we are, any time, we have the capacity to enjoy the sunshine, the presence of each other, and the wonder of our breathing. We don't have to travel anywhere else to do so. We can be in touch with these things right now.

Blaming Never Helps

Blaming has no positive effect at all, nor does trying to persuade using reason and arguments. No blame, no reasoning, no argument, just understanding. If you understand and you show that you understand, you can love, and the situation will change.

Understanding

Understanding and love are not two things, but just one. When you understand, you cannot help but love. You cannot get angry. To develop understanding, you have to practice looking at all living beings with the eyes of compassion. When you understand, you cannot help but love. And when you love, you naturally act in a way that can relieve the suffering of people.

Meditation on Compassion

Love is a mind that brings peace, joy, and happiness to another person. Compassion is a mind that removes the suffering that is present in the other. The essence of love and compassion is understanding, the ability to recognize the physical, material, and psychological suffering of others, to put ourselves "inside the skin" of the other. We "go inside" their body, feelings, and mental formations, and witness for ourselves their suffering. We must become one with the object of our observation.

When we are in contact with another's suffering, a feeling of compassion is born in us. Compassion means, literally, "to suffer with."

Meditation on Love

The mind of love brings peace, joy, and happiness to ourselves and others. If love is real, it will be evident in our daily life, in the way we relate with people and the world.

The source of love is deep in us, and we can help others realize a lot of happiness. One word, one action, or one thought can reduce another person's suffering and bring him joy. One word can give comfort and confidence, destroy doubt, help someone avoid a mistake, reconcile a conflict, or open the door to liberation. One action can save a person's life or help him take advantage of a rare opportunity. One thought can do the same, because thoughts always lead to words and actions. If love is in our heart, every thought, word, and deed can bring about a miracle. Because understanding is the very foundation of love, words and actions that emerge from our love are always helpful.

Investing in Friends

Even if we have a lot of money in the bank, we can die very easily from our suffering. So investing in a friend, making a friend into a real friend, building a community of friends, is a much better source of security. We will have someone to lean on, to come to, during our difficult moments.

We can get in touch with the refreshing, healing elements within and around us thanks to the loving support of other people. If we have a good community of friends, we are very fortunate. To create a good community, we first have to transform ourselves into a good element of the community. After that, we can go to another person and help him or her become an element of the community. We build our network of friends that way. We have to think of friends and community as investments, as our most important asset. They can comfort us and help us in difficult times, and they can share our joy and happiness.

Community of Mindful Living

The foundation of a good community is a daily life that is joyful and happy. Each of us needs to "belong to" a place where each feature of the landscape, the sounds of the bell, and even the buildings are designed to remind us to return to awareness.

The people who live there should emanate peace and freshness, the fruits of living in awareness. They will be like beautiful trees, and the visitors will want to come and sit under their shade. Even when they cannot actually visit, they only need to think of it and smile, and they will feel themselves becoming peaceful and happy.

We can also transform our own family or household into a community that practices harmony and awareness. Together we can practice breathing and smiling, sitting together, drinking tea together in mindfulness. If we have a bell, the bell is also part of the community, because the bell helps us practice. If we have a meditation cushion, the cushion is also part of the community, as there are many other things that help us practice mindfulness, such as the air for breathing. All these efforts can help us establish a community at home. From time to time we can invite a friend to join us. Practicing mindfulness is much easier with a community.

Mindfulness Must Be Engaged

We must be aware of the real problems of the world. Then, with mindfulness, we will know what to do and what not to do to be of help. If we maintain awareness of our breathing and continue to practice smiling, even in difficult situations, many people, animals, and plants will benefit from our way of doing things.

PART THREE

Peace Is Every Step

Interbeing

"Interbeing" is a word that is not in the dictionary yet, but if we combine the prefix "inter-" with the verb "to be," we have a new verb, inter-be.

If we look into this sheet of paper deeply we can see the sunshine in it. Without sunshine, the forest cannot grow. And so, we know that the sunshine is also in this sheet of paper. And if we continue to look, we can see the logger who cut the tree and brought it to the mill to be transformed into paper. And we see wheat. We know that the logger cannot exist without his daily bread, and therefore the wheat that became his bread is also in this sheet of paper. The logger's father and mother are in it too. When we look in this way, we see that without all of these things, this sheet of paper cannot exist.

Looking even more deeply, we can see ourselves in this sheet of paper too because when we look at a sheet of paper, it is part of our perception. Your mind is in here and mine is also. So we can say that everything is in here with this sheet of paper.

Everything co-exists with this sheet of paper. We cannot just *be* by ourselves alone. We have to inter-be with every other thing. This sheet of paper is, because everything else is.

Waging Peace

Many people are aware of the world's suffering; their hearts are filled with compassion. They know what needs to be done, and they engage in political, social, and environmental work to try to change things. But after a period of intense involvement, they may become discouraged if they lack the strength needed to sustain a life of action. Real strength is not in power, money, or weapons, but in deep, inner peace.

Practicing mindfulness in each moment of our daily lives, we can cultivate our own peace. With clarity, determination, and patience—the fruits of meditation—we can sustain a life of action and be real instruments of peace. I have seen this peace in people of various religious and cultural backgrounds who spend their time and energy protecting the weak, struggling for social justice, lessening the disparity between rich and poor, stopping the arms race, fighting against discrimination, and watering the trees of love and understanding throughout the world.

Not Two

When we want to understand something, we cannot just stand outside and observe it. We have to enter deeply into it and be one with it. If we want to understand a person, we have to feel his feelings, suffer his sufferings, and enjoy his joy. In Buddhism, we call this kind of understanding "non-duality." Not two.

Citizenship

As citizens, we have a large responsibility. Meditation is to look deeply into things and to see how we can change ourselves and how we can transform our situation. To transform our situation is also to transform our minds. As we begin to live more responsibly, we must ask our political leaders to move in the same direction. We have to encourage them to stop polluting our environment and our consciousness.

Ecology of Mind

We need harmony, we need peace. Peace is based on respect for life, the spirit of reverence for life. Not only do we have to respect the lives of human beings, but we have to respect the lives of animals, vegetables, and minerals.

Ecology should be a deep ecology. Not only deep but universal, because there is pollution in our consciousness. Television, for instance, is a form of pollution for us and for our children. Television sows seeds of violence and anxiety in our children and pollutes their consciousness, just as we destroy our environment by chemicals, tree-cutting, and polluting the water. We need to protect the ecology of the mind, or this kind of violence and recklessness will continue to spill over into many other areas of life.

The Roots of War

The roots of war are in the way we live our daily lives—the way we develop our industries, build up our society, and consume goods. We have to look deeply into the situation. We cannot just blame one side or the other. We have to transcend the tendency to take sides.

During any conflict, we need people who can understand the suffering of all sides. We need links. We need communication.

Practicing nonviolence is first of all to become nonviolence. Then when a difficult situation presents itself, we will react in a way that will help the situation. This applies to problems of the family as well as to problems of society.

Reconciliation

What can we do when we have hurt people and they consider us to be their enemy? These people might be people in our family, in our community, or in another country. The first thing is to take the time to say, "I am sorry. I hurt you out of my ignorance, out of my lack of mindfulness, out of my lack of skillfulness." The second thing to do is to try to bring out the best part in ourselves to transform ourselves. That is called "speaking with your life and not just with words."

Love in Action

During our journey together, I have presented a number of practices to help us maintain mindfulness of what is going on inside us and immediately around us. Now, as we make our way through the wider world, some additional guidelines can help and protect us. We call them the fourteen precepts of the Order of Interbeing.

1. Do not be idolatrous about or bound to any doctrine, theory, or ideology. All systems of thought are guiding means; they are not absolute truth.

2. *Do not think that the knowledge you presently possess is changeless, absolute truth. Avoid being narrow-minded and bound to present views.*

3. *Do not force others to adopt your views, whether by authority, threat, money, propaganda, or even education.*

4. *Do not avoid contact with suffering or close your eyes before suffering.*

5. *Do not accumulate wealth while millions are hungry. Live simply and*

share time, energy, and material resources with those who are in need.

6. Do not maintain anger or hatred. Learn to penetrate and transform them while they are still seeds in your consciousness. As soon as anger or hatred arises, turn your attention to your breathing in order to see and understand the nature of your anger or hatred and the nature of the persons who have caused your anger or hatred.

7. Do not lose yourself in dispersion and in your surroundings. Practice mindful breathing in order to come back to what is happening in the present moment. Be in touch with what is wondrous, refreshing, and healing, both inside and around yourself.

8. Do not utter words that can create discord and cause the community to break. Make every effort to reconcile and resolve all conflicts, however small.

9. Do not say untruthful things for the sake of personal interest or to impress people. Do not utter words that cause division and hatred. Do not spread news that you do not know to be certain. Do not criticize or condemn things that you are not sure of. Always speak truthfully and constructively.

10. Do not use the religious community for personal gain or profit, or transform your community into a political party.

11. Select a vocation that helps realize your ideal of compassion.

12. Do not kill. Do not let others kill. Find whatever means possible to protect life and prevent war.

13. *Possess nothing that should belong to others. Respect the property of others but prevent others from enriching themselves from human suffering or the suffering of other beings.*

14. *Do not mistreat your body. Learn to handle it with respect. Respect the rights and commitments of others.*

Entering the Twenty-First Century

We need to use the suffering of the twentieth century as compost, so that together we can create flowers for the twenty-first century. The flower of tolerance to see and appreciate cultural diversity is one flower we can cultivate for the children of the twenty-first century. Another flower is the truth of suffering—there has been so much unnecessary suffering in our century. If we are willing to work together and learn together, we can all benefit from the mistakes of our time, and, seeing with the eyes of compassion and understanding, we can offer the next century a beautiful garden and a clear path.

Peace is available in every moment, in every breath, in every step.

I have enjoyed our journey together. I hope you have enjoyed it too. We shall see each other again.